WHO'S THERE?

Knock, knock.
Who's there?
Heidi.
Heidi who?
Heidiclare, this is a funny joke.

* * *

Knock, knock.
Who's there?
Hester.
Hester who?
Hester la vista baby!

* * *

Knock, knock.
Who's there?
Ida.
Ida who?
Ida opened the door long ago.

* * *

Knock, knock.
Who's there?
Ina.
Ina who?
Ina meenie miney mo.

* * *

Knock, knock.
Who's there?
Juanita.
Juanita who?
Juanita big meal.

* * *

Knock, knock.
Who's there?
Jess.
Jess who?
Jess got here a minute late.

* * *

CONTENTS

GOOD CLEAN

KNOCK-KNOCK JOKES

for Kids

BOB PHILLIPS

HARVEST HOUSE PUBLISHERS

EUGENE, OREGON

Cover by Dugan Design Group, Bloomington, Minnesota

Cover illustration © Dugan Design Group

GOOD CLEAN KNOCK-KNOCK JOKES FOR KIDS
Copyright © 2007 by Bob Phillips
Published by Harvest House Publishers
Eugene, Oregon 97402

ISBN-13: 978-0-7369-1778-0
ISBN-10: 0-7369-1778-0

Printed in the United States of America.

08 09 10 11 12 13 14 / BP-SK / 10 9 8 7 6 5 4

Knock, knock.
Who's there?
Poppy.
Poppy who?
Poppy corn with butter tastes good.

* * *

Knock, knock.
Who's there?
Polly.
Polly who?
Polly wants a cracker.

* * *

Knock, knock.
Who's there?
Liz.
Liz who?
Liz see if you can open the door.

* * *

Knock, knock.
Who's there?
Sue.
Sue who?
Sue you later.

* * *

Knock, knock.
Who's there?
June.
June who?
June know how to tell knock-knock jokes?

* * *

Knock, knock.
Who's there?
Fanny.
Fanny who?
Fanny knock-knock joke, isn't it?

* * *

Knock, knock.
Who's there?
Flora.
Flora who?
Flora is what you stand on.

* * *

Knock, knock.
Who's there?
Bea.
Bea who?
Bea good sport and open the door.

* * *

Knock, knock.
Who's there?
Alison.
Alison who?
Alison Wonderland.

* * *

Knock, knock.
Who's there?
Amber.
Amber who?
Ambersting with laughter.

* * *

Knock, knock.
Who's there?
Ada.
Ada who?
Ada lot of pizza last night.

* * *

Knock, knock.
Who's there?
Juno.
Juno who?
Juno how to open the door?

* * *

Knock, knock.
Who's there?
Carmen.
Carmen who?
Carmen 'round the mountain when she comes.

* * *

Knock, knock.
Who's there?
Carrie.
Carrie who?
Carrie me back to old Virginia.

* * *

Knock, knock.
Who's there?
Aurora.
Aurora who?
Aurora borealis.

* * *

Knock, knock.
Who's there?
Celeste.
Celeste who?
Celeste time I'm going to come to your house if you
    don't open the door.

I HEAR A RAPPING SOUND!

Knock, knock.
Who's there?
Vanda.
Vanda who?
Vanda come outside and play ball?

* * *

Knock, knock.
Who's there?
Violet.
Violet who?
Violet the cow out of the barn.

* * *

Knock, knock.
Who's there?
Joan.
Joan who?
Joan call us, we'll call you.

* * *

Knock, knock.
Who's there?
Shirley.
Shirley who?
Shirley you're going to let me in.

* * *

Knock, knock.
Who's there?
Diana.
Diana who?
Diana thirst—a glass of water please!

* * *

Knock, knock.
Who's there?
Debbie.
Debbie who?
Debbie or not, here I come.

* * *

Knock, knock.
Who's there?
Donna.
Donna who?
Donna you know? Open the door and see.

* * *

Knock, knock.
Who's there?
Honor Claire.
Honor Claire who?
Honor Claire day you can see the mountains.

* * *

Knock, knock.
Who's there?
Olive.
Olive who?
Olive to tell knock-knock jokes.

* * *

Knock, knock.
Who's there?
Sharon.
Sharon who?
Sharon your toys is a good thing to do.

* * *

Knock, knock.
Who's there?
Elsie.
Elsie who?
Elsie you tomorrow. I'm getting tired of waiting outside.

* * *

Knock, knock.
Who's there?
Aida.
Aida who?
Aida big piece of watermelon.

* * *

Knock, knock.
Who's there?
Emma.
Emma who?
Emma in town now—how about you?

* * *

Knock, knock.
Who's there?
Colleen.
Colleen who?
Colleen your hands—they are all dirty.

* * *

Knock, knock.
Who's there?
Barbara.
Barbara who?
Barbara black sheep, have you any wool?

❋ ❋ ❋

Knock, knock.
Who's there?
Wendy.
Wendy who?
Wendy day, isn't it?

❋ ❋ ❋

Knock, knock.
Who's there?
Dionne.
Dionne who?
Dionne my last test I took.

❋ ❋ ❋

Knock, knock.
Who's there?
Doughnut.
Doughnut who?
Doughnut you wanna open the door and find out?

❋ ❋ ❋

Knock, knock.
Who's there?
Justin.
Justin who?
Justin time for dinner.

3

SOMEBODY IS AT
THE DOOR!

Knock, knock.
Who's there?
Luke.
Luke who?
Luke through the peephole and find out.

* * *

Knock, knock.
Who's there?
Alexis.
Alexis who?
Alexis is the type of car I drive.

* * *

Knock, knock.
Who's there?
Julie.
Julie who?
Julie the key under the mat?

* * *

Knock, knock.
Who's there?
Phillip.
Phillip who?
Phillip the candy dish—I've got a sweet tooth.

* * *

Knock, knock.
Who's there?
Yah.
Yah who?
What are you so excited about?

* * *

Knock, knock.
Who's there?
Abie.
Abie who?
Abie, C, D, E, F, G, H, I, J, K, L, M, N, O, P, Q, R, S, T,
U, V, W, X, Y, Z.

* * *

Knock, knock.
Who's there?
Yule.
Yule who?
Yule see if you open the door.

* * *

Knock, knock.
Who's there?
Abbie.
Abbie who?
Abbie stung me.

* * *

Knock, knock.
Who's there?
Adair.
Adair who?
Adair you to find out.

* * *

Knock, knock.
Who's there?
Annette.
Annette who?
Annette is a good thing to fish with.

* * *

Knock, knock.
Who's there?
Ben.
Ben who?
Ben here a while…Want to let me in?

* * *

Knock, knock.
Who's there?
Caesar.
Caesar who?
Caesars help you cut things.

* * *

Knock, knock.
Who's there?
Cargo.
Cargo who?
Cargo fast and run over my foot.

* * *

Knock, knock.
Who's there?
Carolyn.
Carolyn who?
Christmas Carolyn is what I'm doing.

* * *

Knock, knock.
Who's there?
Walter.
Walter who?
Walter off a duck's back.

* * *

Knock, knock.
Who's there?
Arthur.
Arthur who?
Arthur any kids who want to come out and play?

* * *

Knock, knock.
Who's there?
Dakota.
Dakota who?
Dakota paint is peeling off of your door.

* * *

Knock, knock.
Who's there?
Ivor.
Ivor who?
Ivor sore hand from knocking on your door.

* * *

Knock, knock.
Who's there?
Dewey.
Dewey who?
Dewey have to go through this routine every time I
    knock on your door?

* * *

Knock, knock.
Who's there?
Noah.
Noah who?
Noah fence, but I'm not going to tell you.

* * *

Knock, knock.
Who's there?
Doris.
Doris who?
Doris open—can I come in?

* * *

Knock, knock.
Who's there?
Hyram.
Hyram who?
Hyram Popeye the Sailor Man.

* * *

Knock, knock.
Who's there?
Noah.
Noah who?
Noah any new knock-knock jokes?

RAP, RAP, RAP!

Knock, knock.
Who's there?
Dusty.
Dusty who?
It's Dusty on your porch…you'd better bring a
   broom.

* * *

Knock, knock.
Who's there?
Snow.
Snow who?
Snow use…I forgot my name.

* * *

Knock, knock.
Who's there?
Hugh.
Hugh who?
Hugh mean to tell to tell me you really don't know?

* * *

Knock, knock.
Who's there?
Norma Lee.
Norma Lee who?
Norma Lee I have my key with me.

* * *

Knock, knock.
Who's there?
Hal.
Hal who?
Hal should I know?

* * *

Knock, knock.
Who's there?
Wendy.
Wendy who?
Wendy joke is over, you had better laugh.

* * *

Knock, knock.
Who's there?
Gladys.
Gladys who?
Gladys me, aren't you?

* * *

Knock, knock.
Who's there?
Sacha.
Sacha who?
Sacha fuss—and just because I knocked at your door!

* * *

Knock, knock.
Who's there?
Hank.
Hank who?
You're welcome.

* * *

Knock, knock.
Who's there?
Len.
Len who?
Len me five bucks, would ya?

* * *

Knock, knock.
Who's there?
Robin.
Robin who?
Robin banks is not a good thing to do.

✳ ✳ ✳

Knock, knock.
Who's there?
Harley.
Harley who?
Harley hear ya…can you speak up?

✳ ✳ ✳

Knock, knock.
Who's there?
Hiram.
Hiram who?
Hiram fine. How are you?

✳ ✳ ✳

Knock, knock.
Who's there?
You.
You who?
Did you call me?

✳ ✳ ✳

Knock, knock.
Who's there?
Ivana.
Ivana who?
Ivana come in! Open the door.

✳ ✳ ✳

Knock, knock.
Who's there?
Seymour.
Seymour who?
Seymour of me if you let me in.

✳ ✳ ✳

Knock, knock.
Who's there?
Atlas.
Atlas who?
Atlas it's Friday, and I'm looking forward to the weekend.

✳ ✳ ✳

Knock, knock.
Who's there?
Boo.
Boo who?
Don't cry. It's only a knock-knock joke.

✳ ✳ ✳

Knock, knock.
Who's there?
Pat.
Pat who?
Pat me on the back. I just won a medal in the track
  meet.

* * *

Knock, knock.
Who's there?
Disk.
Disk who?
Disk is a recorded message.

* * *

Knock, knock.
Who's there?
Lacey.
Lacey who?
Lacey good for nothing.

* * *

Knock, knock.
Who's there?
Dana.
Dana who?
Dana talk with your mouth full.

* * *

Knock, knock.
Who's there?
Kent.
Kent who?
Kent reach the doorbell...that's why I'm knocking.

＊ ＊ ＊

Knock, knock.
Who's there?
Mary Lee.
Mary Lee who?
Mary Lee, Mary Lee, Mary Lee, Mary Lee, life is but
    a dream.

WHO'S OUTSIDE?

Knock, knock.
Who's there?
Theresa.
Theresa who?
Theresa fly in my soup.

* * *

Knock, knock.
Who's there?
Macy.
Macy who?
Macy your driver's license?

* * *

Knock, knock.
Who's there?
Howie.
Howie who?
I'm fine, how are you?

* * *

Knock, knock.
Who's there?
Noah.
Noah who?
Noah good restaurant in this area?

* * *

Knock, knock.
Who's there?
Lisa.
Lisa who?
Lisa you can do is let me in.

* * *

Knock, knock.
Who's there?
Albie.
Albie who?
Albie back!

* * *

Knock, knock.
Who's there?
Dozen.
Dozen who?
Dozen anyone ever answer the door?

* * *

Knock, knock.
Who's there?
Rita.
Rita who?
Rita any good knock-knock jokes lately?

* * *

Knock, knock.
Who's there?
L.B.
L.B. who?
L.B. seeing you later.

* * *

Knock, knock.
Who's there?
Fresno.
Fresno who?
Rudolph the Fresno reindeer.

* * *

Knock, knock.
Who's there?
Gorilla.
Gorilla who?
Gorilla your dreams.

* * *

Knock, knock.
Who's there?
Izzy.
Izzy who?
Izzy come, izzy go.

* * *

Knock, knock.
Who's there?
Far East.
Far East who?
Far East a jolly good fellow.

* * *

Knock, knock.
Who's there?
Carmen.
Carmen who?
Carmen get it!

* * *

Knock, knock.
Who's there?
Nana.
Nana who?
Nana your business.

* * *

Knock, knock.
Who's there?
Colleen.
Colleen who?
Colleen all cars!

* * *

Knock, knock.
Who's there?
Kent.
Kent who?
Kent you just open the door for a change?

* * *

Knock, knock.
Who's there?
Noah.
Noah who?
Noah business like show business.

* * *

Knock, knock.
Who's there?
Razor.
Razor who?
Razor your hands—this is a stick-up!

* * *

Knock, knock.
Who's there?
Missouri.
Missouri who?
Missouri loves company.

* * *

Knock, knock.
Who's there?
Police.
Police who?
Police open the door and let me in.

* * *

Knock, knock.
Who's there?
Reggie.
Reggie who?
Reggie or not, here I come!

* * *

Knock, knock.
Who's there?
Luke.
Luke who?
Luke before you leap.

GO AWAY!

Knock, knock.
Who's there?
Brad.
Brad who?
Brad goes best with peanut butter and jelly.

* * *

Knock, knock.
Who's there?
Carmen.
Carmen who?
Carmen to my arms and give me a hug.

* * *

Knock, knock.
Who's there?
Kipper.
Kipper who?
Kipper your hands to yourself.

* * *

Knock, knock.
Who's there?
Yukon.
Yukon who?
Yukon lead a horse to water, but you can't make
    him drink!

* * *

Knock, knock.
Who's there?
Doughnut.
Doughnut who?
Doughnut forsake me, oh my darling.

* * *

Knock, knock.
Who's there?
Fern.
Fern who?
Fern crying out loud, let me in!

* * *

Knock, knock.
Who's there?
Sabina.
Sabina who?
Sabina long time since I last saw you.

* * *

Knock, knock.
Who's there?
Tennis.
Tennis who?
Tennis the number that comes before eleven.

* * *

Knock, knock.
Who's there?
Zoom.
Zoom who?
Zoom did you expect?

* * *

Knock, knock.
Who's there?
Cashew.
Cashew who?
Cashew see I'm freezing out here?

* * *

Knock, knock.
Who's there?
You.
You who?
You who yourself!

* * *

Knock.
Who's there?
Opportunity.
Opportunity who?
Opportunity knocks but once.

* * *

Knock, knock.
Who's there?
Cedar.
Cedar who?
Join the Navy and cedar world.

* * *

Knock, knock.
Who's there?
Luke.
Luke who?
Luke what the cat dragged in!

* * *

Knock, knock.
Who's there?
New Year.
New Year who?
New Year were gonna ask me that!

* * *

Knock, knock.
Who's there?
Oscar.
Oscar who?
Oscar silly question, get a silly answer.

* * *

Knock, knock.
Who's there?
Rudy.
Hey, I'm Rudy too.
Don't be Rudy to me.

* * *

Knock, knock.
Who's there?
Butcher.
Butcher who?
Butcher money where your mouth is.

* * *

Knock, knock.
Who's there?
Dinah.
Dinah who?
Dinah-saur!

* * *

Knock, knock.
Who's there?
Torch.
Torch who?
Torch you would never ask.

* * *

Knock, knock.
Who's there?
Scold.
Scold who?
Scold outside.

* * *

Knock, knock.
Who's there?
Adair.
Adair who?
Adair once, but now I'm bald.

* * *

Knock, knock.
Who's there?
Halibut.
Halibut who?
Halibut a kiss, dear?

* * *

WHO'S BANGING ON THE DOOR?

Knock, knock.
Who's there?
Jeff.
Jeff who?
Jeff in both ears—please speak up.

* * *

Knock, knock.
Who's there?
Candy.
Candy who?
Candy you come out and play?

* * *

Knock, knock.
Who's there?
Luke.
Luke who?
Luke snappy and open the door.

* * *

Knock, knock.
Who's there?
Freddie.
Freddie who?
Freddie or not, here I come.

* * *

Knock, knock.
Who's there?
Wooden shoe.
Wooden shoe who?
Wooden shoe like to know?

* * *

Knock, knock.
Who's there?
Fido.
Fido who?
Fido known you were coming, I'd have baked a cake!

* * *

Knock, knock.
Who's there?
Howard.
Howard who?
Howard you like to come outside and play?

✳ ✳ ✳

Knock, knock.
Who's there?
Shelby.
Shelby who?
Shelby comin' around the mountain when she comes.

✳ ✳ ✳

Knock, knock.
Who's there?
Aardvark.
Aardvark who?
Aardvark a mile for one of your smiles.

✳ ✳ ✳

Knock, knock.
Who's there?
Franz.
Franz who?
Franz, Romans, countrymen…lend me your ears.

✳ ✳ ✳

Knock, knock.
Who's there?
The owl says.
The owl says who?
Exactly!

* * *

Knock, knock.
Who's there?
Major.
Major who?
Major look, didn't I?

* * *

Knock, knock.
Who's there?
Worm.
Worm who?
Worm in here, isn't it?

* * *

Knock, knock.
Who's there?
Wayne.
Wayne who?
Wayne are you coming over to my house?

* * *

Knock, knock.
Who's there?
Sadie.
Sadie who?
Sadie magic word, and I'll tell you.

* * *

Knock, knock.
Who's there?
Roach.
Roach who?
Roach you a letter…why didn't you write back?

* * *

Knock, knock.
Who's there?
Wayne.
Wayne who?
Wayne are you ever going to open the door?

* * *

Knock, knock.
Who's there?
Igor.
Igor who?
Igor to come inside if you ever open the door.

* * *

Knock, knock.
Who's there?
Butter.
Butter who?
Butter open the door, or I'll huff and puff...and
blow your house in.

I'M COMING!

Knock, knock.
Who's there?
Leif.
Leif who?
Leif me outside, and I'll take my ball and go home.

* * *

Knock, knock.
Who's there?
Xavier.
Xavier who?
Xavier breath…I'm not going to tell you.

* * *

Knock, knock.
Who's there?
Lettuce.
Lettuce who?
Lettuce in, we've been standing out here for a long
time.

* * *

Knock, knock.
Who's there?
Dunce.
Dunce who?
Dunce say anything…just open the door.

* * *

Knock, knock.
Who's there?
Donut.
Donut who?
Donut come near me…I've got a cold.

* * *

Knock, knock.
Who's there?
Turnip.
Turnip who?
Turnip the heat and let me in…I'm freezing.

* * *

Knock, knock.
Who's there?
Walter.
Walter who?
Walter you asking so many questions for?

* * *

Knock, knock.
Who's there?
Omelet.
Omelet who?
Omelet smarter than I look.

* * *

Knock, knock.
Who's there?
Ice cream.
Ice cream who?
Ice cream if you don't let me in.

* * *

Knock, knock.
Who's there?
Celery.
Celery who?
Celery dance in the street?

* * *

Knock, knock.
Who's there?
Stu.
Stu who?
Stu late to ask silly questions.

* * *

Knock, knock.
Who's there?
Attila.
Attila who?
Attila your mother if you don't let me in.

* * *

Knock, knock.
Who's there?
Artichoke.
Artichoke who?
Artichokes when they serve liver for lunch.

* * *

Knock, knock.
Who's there?
Max.
Max who?
Max no difference. Just open the door!

* * *

Knock, knock.
Who's there?
Andy.
Andy who?
Andy dish ran away with the spoon.

* * *

Knock, knock.
Who's there?
Muffin.
Muffin who?
Muffin ventured, muffin gained.

* * *

Knock, knock.
Who's there?
Weirdo.
Weirdo who?
Weirdo you think you're going?

* * *

Knock, knock.
Who's there?
Rose.
Rose who?
Rose, Rose, Rose your boat…gently down the stream.

* * *

Knock, knock.
Who's there?
Olive.
Olive who?
Olive all these knock-knock jokes.

* * *

Knock, knock.
Who's there?
Cello.
Cello who?
Cello. I was just in the neighborhood and thought
  I'd stop by.

* * *

Knock, knock.
Who's there?
Stu.
Stu who?
If the Stu fits…wear it!

* * *

Knock, knock.
Who's there?
Harry.
Harry who?
Harry up and open the door. What's taking you so long?

* * *

Knock, knock.
Who's there?
Weird.
Weird who?
Weird you get such a funny face?

* * *

Knock, knock.
Who's there?
Yukon.
Yukon who?
Yukon say that again.

STOP THAT BANGING!

Knock, knock.
Who's there?
Hedda.
Hedda who?
My Hedda hurts...do you have any asprin?

* * *

Knock, knock.
Who's there?
Crypt.
Crypt who?
Crypt up to your door to see if you were home.

* * *

Knock, knock.
Who's there?
Warrior.
Warrior who?
Warrior you been all of my life?

* * *

Knock, knock.
Who's there?
Hope.
Hope who?
Hope you can come out and play ball.

* * *

Knock, knock.
Who's there?
Goblin.
Goblin who?
Goblin your food is not good manners.

* * *

Knock, knock.
Who's there?
Stopwatch.
Stopwatch who?
Stopwatch you're doing and open the door.

* * *

Knock, knock.
Who's there?
Ray.
Ray who?
No, Hoo-Ray.

* * *

Knock, knock.
Who's there?
Ooze.
Ooze who?
Ooze going to change the baby's diaper?

* * *

Knock, knock.
Who's there?
Heart.
Heart who?
Heart to hear you…talk louder.

* * *

Knock, knock.
Who's there?
Pancho.
Pancho who?
Pancho lights out if you don't let me in.

* * *

Knock, knock.
Who's there?
Oliver.
Oliver who?
Oliver sudden I can't remember.

* * *

Knock, knock.
Who's there?
Sicily.
Sicily who?
Ask a Sicily question and get a Sicily answer.

* * *

Knock, knock.
Who's there?
Alfredo.
Alfredo who?
Are you Alfredo the big bad wolf?

* * *

Knock, knock.
Who's there?
Sultan.
Sultan who?
Please pass the Sultan pepper.

* * *

Knock, knock.
Who's there?
Irish.
Irish who?
Irish I knew.

* * *

Knock, knock.
Who's there?
Ooze.
Ooze who?
Ooze in charge around here?

* * *

Knock, knock.
Who's there?
Vanna.
Vanna who?
Vanna make something of it?

* * *

Knock, knock.
Who's there?
Ilona.
Ilona who?
Ilona Ranger and Tonto.

* * *

Knock, knock.
Who's there?
Wanda.
Wanda who?
Wanda go to the movies?

* * *

Knock, knock.
Who's there?
Your mom.
Your mom who?
Very funny, now let me in.

* * *

Knock, knock.
Who's there?
Your dad.
Your dad who?
Your dad who's going to give you a spanking if you
    don't open the door.

* * *

Knock, knock.
Who's there?
Disaster.
Disaster who?
Disaster be my lucky day.

* * *

Knock, knock.
Who's there?
Account.
Account who?
Account on my fingers and toes.

10

I'M NOT OPENING
THE DOOR!

Knock, knock.
Who's there?
Pasture.
Pasture who?
I think it's Pasture bedtime.

* * *

Knock, knock.
Who's there?
Acorn.
Acorn who?
Acorn give you anything but love, baby.

* * *

Knock, knock.
Who's there?
Gladys.
Gladys who?
Gladys summer vacation…how about you?

* * *

Knock, knock.
Who's there?
Acme.
Acme who?
Acme again and I'll tell you the same thing.

* * *

Knock, knock.
Who's there?
Who.
Who who?
You sound like an owl.

* * *

Knock, knock.
Who's there?
Al.
Al who?
Al be down to get you in a taxi.

* * *

Knock, knock.
Who's there?
Theodore.
Theodore who?
Theodore is closed…open up!

* * *

Knock, knock.
Who's there?
Adore.
Adore who?
Adore is what I've been knocking on.

* * *

Knock, knock.
Who's there?
Jewel.
Jewel who?
Jewel remember me. I'm the one who keeps
    knocking at your door.

* * *

Knock, knock.
Who's there?
Alaska.
Alaska who?
Alaska to come in the back door next time.

* * *

Knock, knock.
Who's there?
Major.
Major who?
Major open the door, didn't I?

* * *

Knock, knock.
Who's there?
Adolf.
Adolf who?
Adolf ball hit me in the mowf.

* * *

Knock, knock.
Who's there?
Altoona.
Altoona who?
Altoona my car so it will run better.

* * *

Knock, knock.
Who's there?
Ears.
Ears who?
Ears another knock-knock joke for you.

* * *

Knock, knock.
Who's there?
Anson.
Anson who?
Anson my pants are making me jump around.

* * *

Knock, knock.
Who's there?
Noah.
Noah who?
Noahbody knows.

* * *

Knock, knock.
Who's there?
Anita.
Anita who?
Anita come inside for a sandwich.

* * *

Knock, knock.
Who's there?
Answer.
Answer who?
Answer everywhere in our house.

* * *

Knock, knock.
Who's there?
Ansel.
Ansel who?
Ansel bite you if you're not careful.

* * *

Knock, knock.
Who's there?
Congo.
Congo who?
Congo on knocking at your door forever.

* * *

Knock, knock.
Who's there?
Arch.
Arch who?
Arch you glad you're inside?

* * *

Knock, knock.
Who's there?
Dawn.
Dawn who?
Dawn do anything I wouldn't do.

THE DOOR IS SHUT!

Knock, knock.
Who's there?
Aroma.
Aroma who?
Aroma round your front yard.

* * *

Knock, knock.
Who's there?
Dennis.
Dennis who?
Dennis, anyone?

* * *

Knock, knock.
Who's there?
Athena.
Athena who?
Athena elephant at the circus.

* * *

Knock, knock.
Who's there?
Dewey.
Dewey who?
Dewey have to listen to any more knock-knock jokes?

* * *

Knock, knock.
Who's there?
Aurora.
Aurora who?
Aurora is what lions and tigers do.

* * *

Knock, knock.
Who's there?
Wah.
Wah who?
I didn't know you were a cowboy.

* * *

Knock, knock.
Who's there?
Avenue.
Avenue who?
Avenue anything better to do than listen to knock-
    knock jokes?

* * *

Knock, knock.
Who's there?
Theophilus.
Theophilus who?
These are Theophilus knock-knock jokes I've ever heard.

* * *

Knock, knock.
Who's there?
Banana split.
Banana split who?
Banana split when she saw the monkey coming.

* * *

Knock, knock.
Who's there?
Upton.
Upton who?
Upton now I've enjoyed telling knock-knock jokes.

* * *

Knock, knock.
Who's there?
Barley.
Barley who?
I barley know what to say.

* * *

Knock, knock.
Who's there?
Juicy.
Juicy who?
Juicy who threw that baseball through the window?

* * *

Knock, knock.
Who's there?
Bat.
Bat who?
Bat you'll never figure it out.

* * *

Knock, knock.
Who's there?
Madam.
Madam who?
Madam and Eve ate the forbidden fruit.

* * *

Knock, knock.
Who's there?
Batten.
Batten who?
Batten down the hatches—a storm is coming.

* * *

Knock, knock.
Who's there?
Macron.
Macron who?
Macron pancakes for breakfast.

* * *

Knock, knock.
Who's there?
Battle.
Battle who?
Battle fly out of the cave at night.

* * *

Knock, knock.
Who's there?
Lux.
Lux who?
Lux like we're locked out of the house.

* * *

Knock, knock.
Who's there?
Begonia.
Begonia who?
Begonia pardon but you have bad breath.

* * *

Knock, knock.
Who's there?
Lucy.
Lucy who?
Lucy Goosey and Henny Penny.

* * *

Knock, knock.
Who's there?
Bison.
Bison who?
Bison ice cream and let me have some.

* * *

Knock, knock.
Who's there?
Lucas.
Lucas who?
Lucas up next time you come to town.

* * *

Knock, knock.
Who's there?
Boycott.
Boycott who?
Boycott is where small male children sleep.

* * *

Knock, knock.
Who's there?
Luke.
Luke who?
Luke out the window and see.

WHAT'S THAT DRUMMING SOUND?

Knock, knock.
Who's there?
Boyds.
Boyds who?
Boyds fly up in the sky.

* * *

Knock, knock.
Who's there?
Lovitt.
Lovitt who?
Lovitt or leave it.

* * *

Knock, knock.
Who's there?
Buckle.
Buckle who?
Buckle up your seat belt or you'll get a ticket.

* * *

Knock, knock.
Who's there?
Loehmann.
Loehmann who?
A Loehmann is someone who is very short.

* * *

Knock, knock.
Who's there?
Bustle.
Bustle who?
Bustle be picking you up for school.

* * *

Knock, knock.
Who's there?
Lois.
Lois who?
Lois man on the totem pole.

* * *

Knock, knock.
Who's there?
Butcher.
Butcher who?
A butcher is someone who cuts meat in the market.

* * *

Knock, knock.
Who's there?
Lisa.
Lisa who?
Lisa's car costs lots of money.

* * *

Knock, knock.
Who's there?
Canal.
Canal who?
Canal come to my birthday party?

* * *

Knock, knock.
Who's there?
Lightning.
Lightning who?
Lightning bugs like to fly at night.

* * *

Knock, knock.
Who's there?
Canoe.
Canoe who?
Canoe come outside and play?

* * *

Knock, knock.
Who's there?
Lexus.
Lexus who?
Lexus get our act together.

* * *

Knock, knock.
Who's there?
Can't chew.
Can't chew who?
Can't chew stop telling these crazy knock-knock jokes?

* * *

Knock, knock.
Who's there?
Leonie.
Leonie who?
Leonie reason I tell these jokes is to get a smile.

* * *

Knock, knock.
Who's there?
Cello.
Cello who?
Cello. I'm glad to meet you.

* * *

Knock, knock.
Who's there?
Leif.
Leif who?
Leif me a key when you lock the door.

* * *

Knock, knock.
Who's there?
Cargo.
Cargo who?
Cargo down the road without its lights on.

* * *

Knock, knock.
Who's there?
Lecture.
Lecture who?
Lecture go inside first.

* * *

Knock, knock.
Who's there?
CD.
CD who?
CD doorknob? Turn the handle and let me in.

* * *

Knock, knock.
Who's there?
Launch.
Launch who?
Launch is when I eat tuna sandwiches.

* * *

Knock, knock.
Who's there?
Cement.
Cement who?
Cement to be a clever girl.

* * *

Knock, knock.
Who's there?
Lattice.
Lattice who?
I like lattice and tomatoes on my hamburger.

* * *

Knock, knock.
Who's there?
Census.
Census who?
Census raining, I can't play outside with you.

* * *

Knock, knock.
Who's there?
Lass.
Lass who?
Lass but not least.

13

ANYBODY HOME?

Knock, knock.
Who's there?
Center.
Center who?
Center a Valentine card yesterday.

* * *

Knock, knock.
Who's there?
Knotting.
Knotting who?
Knotting ventured, knotting gained.

* * *

Knock, knock.
Who's there?
Cheddar.
Cheddar who?
Cheddar watch out…I'm going to kick your door down.

* * *

Knock, knock.
Who's there?
Kyle.
Kyle who?
Kyle be looking forward to seeing you.

* * *

Knock, knock.
Who's there?
Cinch.
Cinch who?
Cinch you're so nosy, I'm not going to tell you.

* * *

Knock, knock.
Who's there?
Klaus.
Klaus who?
Klaus the door…were you born in a barn?

* * *

Knock, knock.
Who's there?
Consult.
Consult who?
Consult be put on the popcorn?

* * *

Knock, knock.
Who's there?
Damall.
Damall who?
Damall is where I like to go shopping.

* * *

Knock, knock.
Who's there?
Justice.
Justice who?
Justice once—stop telling knock-knock jokes.

* * *

Knock, knock.
Who's there?
Damascus.
Damascus who?
Damascus what you wear for Halloween.

* * *

Knock, knock.
Who's there?
Juno.
Juno who?
Juno the name of the president of the United States?

* * *

Knock, knock.
Who's there?
Darrell.
Darrell who?
Darrell be an ice cream cone for you if you open
the door.

* * *

Knock, knock.
Who's there?
Juan.
Juan who?
Juan day my prince will come.

* * *

Knock, knock.
Who's there?
Decode.
Decode who?
Decode is in my nose.

* * *

Knock, knock.
Who's there?
Joel.
Joel who?
Joel never guess.

* * *

Knock, knock.
Who's there?
Design.
Design who?
Design says "Wet Paint–Do Not Touch."

* * *

Knock, knock.
Who's there?
Jimmy.
Jimmy who?
Jimmy a break and open the door.

* * *

Knock, knock.
Who's there?
Despise.
Despise who?
Despise work for the CIA.

* * *

Knock, knock.
Who's there?
Jet.
Jet who?
Jet little ole me.

* * *

Knock, knock.
Who's there?
Details.
Details who?
Details are what were cut off of the Three Blind Mice.

* * *

Knock, knock.
Who's there?
Jester.
Jester who?
Jester day the sun was shining, and now it's raining.

* * *

Knock, knock.
Who's there?
Devote.
Devote who?
Devote is what the president needs to win the election.

WHO'S TAPPING AT THE DOOR?

Knock, knock.
Who's there?
Jason.
Jason who?
My dog keeps Jason his tail.

* * *

Knock, knock.
Who's there?
Disguise.
Disguise who?
Disguise making me mad for not opening the door.

* * *

Knock, knock.
Who's there?
Jamaica.
Jamaica who?
Jamaica me laugh with all of these knock-knock jokes.

* * *

Knock, knock.
Who's there?
Dewayne.
Dewayne who?
Dewayne fell on Noah's Ark for 40 days and 40 nights.

* * *

Knock, knock.
Who's there?
Jake.
Jake who?
Jake your feet off of my table.

* * *

Knock, knock.
Who's there?
Dishes.
Dishes who?
Dishes a funny knock-knock joke.

* * *

Knock, knock.
Who's there?
Jackal.
Jackal who?
Jackal Jill went up the hill to fetch a pail of water.

✳ ✳ ✳

Knock, knock.
Who's there?
Donahue.
Donahue who?
Donahue want to know who is standing outside
    knocking on your door?

✳ ✳ ✳

Knock, knock.
Who's there?
Issue.
Issue who?
Issue the person who owns the house?

✳ ✳ ✳

Knock, knock.
Who's there?
Donatella.
Donatella who?
Please Donatella any more knock-knock jokes. I
    can't stand it.

✳ ✳ ✳

Knock, knock.
Who's there?
Ivory.
Ivory who?
Ivory time I knock, you never open the door.

* * *

Knock, knock.
Who's there?
Dragon.
Dragon who?
School keeps dragon on and on. When is summer
    vacation?

* * *

Knock, knock.
Who's there?
Indy.
Indy who?
Indy day that you open the door, I'll be glad.

* * *

Knock, knock.
Who's there?
Earl.
Earl who?
Earl be a monkey's uncle.

* * *

Knock, knock.
Who's there?
Ima.
Ima who?
Ima glad you like knock-knock jokes.

* * *

Knock, knock.
Who's there?
Ease.
Ease who?
Ease are part of the alphabet and are followed by F's.

* * *

Knock, knock.
Who's there?
IHOP.
IHOP who?
IHOP you will have a good day.

* * *

Knock, knock.
Who's there?
Easy.
Easy who?
Easy come, easy go.

* * *

Knock, knock.
Who's there?
Iguana.
Iguana who?
Iguana come in but you won't let me.

* * *

Knock, knock.
Who's there?
Eclipse.
Eclipse who?
Eclipse my toenails.

* * *

Knock, knock.
Who's there?
Ida.
Ida who?
Ida know, do you?

* * *

Knock, knock.
Who's there?
Eggs.
Eggs who?
Eggs it...is how you leave the building.

* * *

Knock, knock.
Who's there?
Icon.
Icon who?
Icon see you through the keyhole.

* * *

Knock, knock.
Who's there?
Ego.
Ego who?
Ego fast on a skateboard.

15

USE THE DOORBELL!

Knock, knock.
Who's there?
Eileen Dover.
Eileen Dover who?
Eileen Dover and fell on my nose.

* * *

Knock, knock.
Who's there?
Hummus.
Hummus who?
Hummus be a very funny person.

* * *

Knock, knock.
Who's there?
Hummus.
Hummus who?
Hummus put an end to these silly jokes.

✳ ✳ ✳

Knock, knock.
Who's there?
Ely.
Ely who?
"Ely, Ely, O!"

✳ ✳ ✳

Knock, knock.
Who's there?
Huguenot.
Huguenot who?
Huguenot as smart as I thought you were.

✳ ✳ ✳

Knock, knock.
Who's there?
Equalize.
Equalize who?
Equalize is when both of your eyes are the same size.

✳ ✳ ✳

Knock, knock.
Who's there?
Hoboken.
Hoboken who?
Hoboken the doorbell?

* * *

Knock, knock.
Who's there?
Ewe.
Ewe who?
Are ewe calling for me?

* * *

Knock, knock.
Who's there?
Fangs.
Fangs who?
Fangs for the memory.

* * *

Knock, knock.
Who's there?
Hiram.
Hiram who?
Hiram somebody to mow your lawn.

* * *

Knock, knock.
Who's there?
Foe.
Foe who?
Foe comes after fee and fie and before fum.

* * *

Knock, knock.
Who's there?
High Lava.
High Lava who?
High Lava to tell knock-knock jokes.

* * *

Knock, knock.
Who's there?
Fleece.
Fleece who?
Fleece open the door.

* * *

Knock, knock.
Who's there?
Hewlett.
Hewlett who?
Hewlett you out of the crazy house?

* * *

Knock, knock.
Who's there?
Folly.
Folly who?
Folly wants a cracker.

* * *

Knock, knock.
Who's there?
Hedda.
Hedda who?
Hedda enough of you ignoring my knocking.

* * *

Knock, knock.
Who's there?
Florida.
Florida who?
Florida last time…go knock on someone else's door.

* * *

Knock, knock.
Who's there?
Heaven.
Heaven who?
Heaven a good time yet?

* * *

Knock, knock.
Who's there?
Forest.
Forest who?
Forest the number before five.

* * *

Knock, knock.
Who's there?
Harold.
Harold who?
It's your birthday. Harold will you be?

16

POUND, POUND, POUND!

Knock, knock.
Who's there?
Foy.
Foy who?
Foy the last time, I'm tired of knock-knock jokes.

$$* * *$$

Knock, knock.
Who's there?
Harmony.
Harmony who?
Harmony times do I have to keep knocking?

$$* * *$$

Knock, knock.
Who's there?
Harmony.
Harmony who?
Harmony times do I have to listen to these wacky jokes?

* * *

Knock, knock.
Who's there?
Fraiser.
Fraiser who?
Fraiser jolly good fellow.

* * *

Knock, knock.
Who's there?
Hallways.
Hallways who?
Hallways cover your mouth when you cough.

* * *

Knock, knock.
Who's there?
Friar.
Friar who?
Friar up some hamburgers and hot dogs.

* * *

Knock, knock.
Who's there?
Habit.
Habit who?
Habit you and I go shopping at the mall?

* * *

Knock, knock.
Who's there?
Fuel.
Fuel who?
Fuel open the door, I'll bring you a present.

* * *

Knock, knock.
Who's there?
Gwen.
Gwen who?
Gwen the red, red robin comes bob, bob, bobbin' along.

* * *

Knock, knock.
Who's there?
Gas.
Gas who?
I give up...who?

* * *

Knock, knock.
Who's there?
Groom.
Groom who?
There's plenty of groom for more.

* * *

Knock, knock.
Who's there?
Genial.
Genial who?
Genial go back into the lamp if you ask him nicely.

* * *

Knock, knock.
Who's there?
Gotham.
Gotham who?
Gotham chewing gum for me?

* * *

Knock, knock.
Who's there?
Gideon.
Gideon who?
Gideon up is what you say to horses.

* * *

Knock, knock.
Who's there?
Gosset.
Gosset who?
Gosset down—you're blocking my view.

* * *

Knock, knock.
Who's there?
Gladys.
Gladys who?
Gladys almost summer vacation.

* * *

Knock, knock.
Who's there?
Godiva.
Godiva who?
Godiva in the swimming pool.

* * *

Knock, knock.
Who's there?
Goblin.
Goblin who?
Goblin cake and ice cream is fun.

* * *

Knock, knock.
Who's there?
Goat.
Goat who?
Goat to run. I hear the fire alarm.

* * *

Knock, knock.
Who's there?
Gus.
Gus who?
Gus whose coming for dinner?

* * *

Knock, knock.
Who's there?
Gnome.
Gnome who?
Gnome sweet gnome.

* * *

Knock, knock.
Who's there?
Hair.
Hair who?
Hair today and gone tomorrow.

* * *

Knock, knock.
Who's there?
Glisten.
Glisten who?
Glisten and I will tell you some great knock-knock
    jokes.

* * *

Knock, knock.
Who's there?
Hamal.
Hamal who?
Hamal crackers taste good.

Other Books by Bob Phillips

For more information, send a self-addressed stamped envelope to:

Family Services
P.O. Box 9363
Fresno, California 93702